Virtual Reality in Tourism

Explore the Globe without Leaving Home

Table of Contents

Chapter 1. Introduction

Welcome to an exhilarating new world where your travel dreams no longer know any bounds! In our upcoming Special Report titled 'Virtual Reality in Tourism: Explore the Globe without Leaving Home,' we venture into the exciting intersection of technology and travel. We empower you with the technology to meander through the serenely beautiful Venetian canals, breathe in the unmistakably vibrant essence of New Orleans, or marvel at the breathtakingly majestic Northern Lights - all within the comfort of your home. Our special report is a comprehensive guide and an absolute must-have for tech-savvy explorers and cooped-up homebodies alike, as we seek to revolutionize your perception of travel. Come join us on this virtual expedition to make your globe-trotting dreams a reality!

Chapter 2. Entering the Era of Virtual Tourism

The dawn of the 21st century introduced revolutionary changes in technology that have fundamentally altered the way we travel and experience the world. From GPS navigation and online bookings to user reviews and tips, technology has made travel much more accessible and personalized than ever before. But the real game-changer lies ahead of us: Virtual Reality (VR), and its transformative capacity to obliterate the very boundaries of space and time, merging the physical and the digital like never before.

2.1. Introducing Virtual Tourism

Virtual tourism, powered by VR, is a new form of travel experience that allows you to explore any corner of the world without actually being there. It turns your living room into a serene Buddhist temple in Japan, your study into an opulent art gallery in France, or your backyard into a tropical rainforest in Australia. The application of VR in tourism transcends the physical limitations of distance, cost, health issues, or travel bans. A pair of VR goggles is all you need to become a world explorer, stepping into any city, landmark, or natural wonder, at any time, from any place.

2.2. The Meteoric Rise of VR in Tourism

VR technology isn't exactly new. It has been popular in the gaming industry for quite some time. However, its potential to alter our travel experiences was largely untapped until a few years ago. This has greatly changed in the post-pandemic era, with an exponential increase in the use of VR for tourism purposes.

The boost is primarily driven by a growing user-end demand for immersive, interactive experiences from the safety of our homes, coupled with significant technological advancements. It is estimated that by 2025, the global VR market in tourism will skyrocket, creating an entirely new sector born out of the amalgamation of technology and travel.

2.3. VR's Role in Revolutionizing Travel Experiences

The magic of virtual tourism lies in its ability to provide immersive travel experiences. Gone are the days when travel visits were confined to viewing images or video clips on a flat screen. VR tourism recreates lifelike, multi-dimensional panoramic views that truly make you feel like you are there in person. It does more than merely showing you a place; it makes you experience it.

For instance, when 'visiting' the Great Barrier Reef through VR, you won't just see beautiful imagery of the marine life and the coral reef; you'll feel as if you are diving deep underneath, surrounded by fishes, against the backdrop of the coral reef. Such powerful experiences, previously limited to physical travel, can now be re-lived over and over again, right from your living room.

2.4. The Changing Landscape of Tourism

In addition to individuals, various organizations, destinations, and attractions are readily adopting VR technologies, creating virtual tours to attract the global audience. UNESCO World Heritage Sites, national parks, museums, zoos, and art galleries are using VR to generate virtual tours of their properties. These immersive digital experiences have redefined the concept of visitor engagement and accessibility, imparting education, and preserving the cultural and natural heritage of our world.

Cities like Paris, New York, and Tokyo, known for their bustling streets and iconic landmarks, are offering 360-degree VR experiences. Users can tour these cities, feel the hustle and bustle, admire the architecture, and experience the unique vibe and culture of each city all from the comfort of their home.

2.5. The Future of Virtual Tourism

While there is a world of opportunities for VR in tourism, we are just scratching the surface. As the technology improves further, we will transition from technically augmented visits today to virtually realistic explorations tomorrow, where the line between physical and virtual travel will blur.

Imagine 'booking' a trip to Mars or journeying to historical eras – the possibilities are boundless! VR provides opportunities to travel not just across space but time as well. It is likely that more than just a tool for exploration, VR will become a key platform for storytelling, where we can experience history, art, culture, and science in ways unimaginable today.

In a world advancing rapidly towards digitalization, the globalization of VR tourism will soon be a reality. Inspired by the fusion of fantasy and reality, we are embarking on a journey where traveling the world is no longer a privilege limited to the few but an experience accessible to all.

The era of virtual tourism has arrived, challenging the way we perceive our world and our place in it. With VR, we are not just observers, but active participants in a personalized, engaging, and enlightening journey across the globe. So grab your VR headset and get ready to discover a world without borders, in the truest sense of the word!

Chapter 3. The Science Behind Virtual Reality: An Easy Guide

Virtual Reality (VR) may be a novel concept for some, but it's grounded in a combination of technologies that have been developing and merging over several decades. The science behind it is as compelling as the experiences it delivers, allowing us to be transported to different worlds right from our couches.

3.1. What is Virtual Reality?

Virtual Reality is an immersive computer-generated simulation that provides a 360-degree view, tricking the brain into believing it's somewhere else. Interaction within these virtual environments is feasible through sophisticated electronic equipment, such as specialized gloves and headsets.

3.2. Components of Virtual Reality

There are several key components that create a VR experience: - Virtual World: A simulated environment created by a computer that appears to be from the real or imagined universe. - Immersion: A sensation of being physically present in a non-physical world. - Sensory Feedback: This consists of visual and auditory feedback and can also involve other sensory feedback such as haptic (touch) or olfactory (smell). - Interactive Engagement: Users should be able to interact and influence the environment in a meaningful way.

3.3. The Hardware

Understanding the science behind VR also requires understanding the hardware. Let's delve into a couple of main pieces.

3.3.1. VR Headsets

VR headsets are the most identifiable part of a VR system. They work by displaying two slightly different angles of the scene to each eye, simulating depth. This is, in essence, how depth perception works in our eyes. The headset tracks the user's head motion and the embedded software adjusts the images accordingly, giving the user a seamless 360-degree look at the virtual environment.

3.3.2. Tracking Systems

Head tracking, hand tracking, and eye tracking are vital for creating a convincing VR experience. The tracking systems use sensors, cameras, or other technologies such as lasers to track the user's movements and translate them into the VR scenario in real-time. For instance, if you move your hands or tilt your head, the VR environment will respond accordingly for a seamless experience.

3.4. The Software

Equally important as hardware, the software in VR systems creates the realistic environments that you interact with. The virtual environments created range from the extremely realistic, such as photorealistic renderings of actual cities, to the purely fantastical, like alien worlds.

3.4.1. Rendering

Rendering is generating a photorealistic 2D image or animation from a 3D model. The algorithm for rendering can be programmed to simulate a wide range of natural and artificial phenomena. VR rendering needs to be done at a higher frame rate than is typically required for regular video games or 3D visualizations to ensure a seamless experience.

3.4.2. Physics Engine

To make the virtual world interact in a way that is consistent with the user's expectations and real-world physics, VR utilizes a physics engine. This software simulates and predicts the physical properties of a virtual environment (like gravity, fluid dynamics, and the mechanics of solid objects) for a more immersive experience.

3.5. Bringing it all Together

When combined together, the hardware and software of VR systems create not just a visually immersive environment, but a wholly sensory and interactive experience. The result - a convincing, immersive virtual environment that can be explored and interacted with, effectively fooling the brain into believing that it's somewhere else.

As technology continues to improve and evolve, there's no telling how the landscape of Virtual Reality will expand. But one thing is certain – our ability to explore new places through VR technology is just beginning. After all, the best journeys answer questions we didn't even think to ask. Welcome to your new reality!

Chapter 4. Tourism Reimagined: How VR Transports You Anywhere

Tourism, through the ages, has been an ever-evolving sector, with technology playing an increasingly crucial role. At this juncture, we have an unprecedented opportunity to don the cap of an explorer without the hindrances of time, distance, or physical limitations. This is where Virtual Reality (VR) comes into play – a nuanced technology that holds the potential to immerse us in any part of the world without leaving home.

4.1. The Evolution of Virtual Reality

Turn back the clock a few decades, and VR was nothing more than an imaginative concept in sci-fi books and the dreams of techno-visionaries. The term 'Virtual Reality' was popularized in the late 20th century through the seminal works of Jaron Lanier and his VPL Research.

While an intriguing novelty at first, advances in computing power, sensor technologies, and graphics processing over the ensuing years have rendered it a practical tool for various industries, including tourism. Technologies that once seemed like a pipe dream, such as Oculus Rift, HTC Vive, and Sony PlayStation VR, now sit comfortably in our living rooms, opening a world of possibilities.

4.2. How Virtual Reality Works

Virtual Reality works by simulating our surroundings in a virtual environment. Users wear a unique headset that tracks their head movements and displays a 3D computer-generated environment to their eyes. Additional peripherals, like gloves or controllers, track hand movements and offer avenues for interactivity.

To create an immersive environment, the VR system relies on key elements: a stereoscopic display for depth perception, a tracking system for real-time user movements, and a high refresh rate to ensure seamless motion. The amalgamation of these components creates an illusion of being in a different reality, hence the term 'virtual reality.'

4.3. Redefining Tourism Through VR

For the tourism industry, VR presents a unique opportunity to provide an immersive experience of a location without necessitating travel. Tour operators can deploy VR to showcase attractions and validate the traveler's experience before booking. It enables sight-seeing of distant locales, historical recreations, or even inaccessible locations.

Imagine stepping into a gondola and drifting down the canal paths of Venice all while lounging on your couch, or walking down the bustling narrow lanes of Marrakech soaking in the flavors and scents from the local marketplace, without worrying about travel advisories or ecological footprints.

4.4. VR Tourism: Current Applications

Numerous tourism boards and private companies around the globe have already embraced VR. Thomas Cook, a British travel company, instituted 'try before you fly' VR experiences for customers, which reportedly led to a significant increase in bookings.

Far from the glossy images and strategic angles of photographs, VR gives potential travelers an honest, unfiltered image of what awaits them. Additionally, it serves as an efficient marketing tool for lesser-known destinations, encouraging curiosity and exploration beyond the usual tourist trails.

4.5. Limitations and Future Potential

However, VR is not without its limitations. High costs, the need for significant technical know-how, and the absence of social connectivity can be deterrents for some potential users. Moreover, the technology has yet to mature fully, and as a result, the experiences are not always perfect. Some users report motion sickness and discomfort, which can diminish the virtual experience.

Despite these challenges, the potential of VR tourism is vast. With constant advances in technology, the refinement and penetration of VR gear will continue, making it more accessible and user-friendly. The COVID-19 pandemic has also underscored the need for such solutions, enabling safe, virtual travel at a time when physical mobility is limited.

In the future, we can expect VR tourism to enrich with more sensory inputs - think tactile feedback or smell, adding further layers of depth to the experience.

4.6. Conclusion

There is an African proverb that states, "Until the lion learns how to write, every story will glorify the hunter." In the context of VR in tourism, 'writing' represents the ability of this technology to tell a story holistically, one that encapsulates and respects the fabric of a place rather than merely glorifying it.

While VR tourism will never replace the thrill and connection of physical travel, it can undoubtedly complement it, facilitate informed decision-making and provide an alternative for those for whom travel may not be readily available.

We stand on the precipice of a brave new world ready to explore. VR offers an interactive window into these worlds, a personal looking glass into the experiences we've yearned for. The world is indeed at your fingertips and with virtual reality, we can go anywhere at any time!

Chapter 5. Creating Virtual Worlds: Famous Landmarks in VR

In an era when technology and imagination fuse seamlessly, the world of virtual reality (VR) gifts us the ability to explore famous landmarks from across the globe without leaving the confines of our homes. Aided by high-quality, immersive 3D models and 360-degree imagery, the following sections unravel how VR is recreating bucket-list destinations, at the click of a button or the slip of a headset.

5.1. An exploration into Virtual Reality technology

Virtual Reality generally implies a computer-generated environment, created using software that can be explored and interacted with by an individual. The individual becomes part of this artificial world and is immersed into its reality, often capable of manipulating objects or performing actions.

To achieve this phenomenal experience, you need two main components: a software which builds the Virtual Environment and a hardware which enables interaction with that. The most common VR hardware is the Head Mounted Display (HMD). Essentially goggles, they offer separate images for each eye, stereoscopic display that provides a perception of depth, and a broad field of view to mimic reality. They are often complemented by headphones, hand controllers, and motion detectors to enhance the interactive experience.

Software, often a detailed 3D computer model of a location, uses data collected from various sources like satellite imagery, photogrammetry, traditional mapping databases etc. Advanced computer algorithms then render these models into fully explorable VR environments.

5.2. Virtually visiting the Egyptian Pyramids

One of such wonders emulated in VR is the magnificent Egyptian Pyramids, primarily the Great Pyramid of Giza. To build this experience, data collected from LiDAR scanning was used to map the pyramid's structure, coupled with high resolution photos for texture and authenticity.

Users can now explore the Pyramid from a unique perspective otherwise impossible, like a bird's eye view or from within the pyramid itself. Details from the hieroglyphics on the walls, to the grandeur of the Pharaoh's chamber, are astonishingly accurate.

5.3. A stroll through the Roman Colosseum

The software for this landmark utilized photogrammetry, where a multitude of photographs, taken from varied perspectives, are compiled to build a detailed 3D model of the Roman amphitheater. The VR Roman Colosseum not only lets users roam in and around the architecture, but also travel back in time to experience the grand spectacles held there, complete with the deafening cheer of the virtual crowd.

5.4. Immersing in New York's Times Square

An amalgamation of satellite imagery, street view data and photogrammetry create an astoundingly similar virtual representation of Times Square. From the hustle and bustle of tourists, to the radiant advertising billboards, a trip here is like stepping into the heart of New York City itself.

5.5. Cruising the Canals of Venice

Using data from 3D mapping and photorealistic rendering, virtual travelers can take a serene gondola ride through the canals of Venice. One can admire the intricate architecture of the Palazzo Ducale or simply absorb the splendor of sunset by the Ponte di Rialto.

5.6. The Wonders of the Improbable

In addition to mirroring reality, VR also sheds the constraints of physics and feasibility. Fancy having a rendezvous atop Everest? Or soak in the ethereal beauty of Aurora Borealis from outer space? The realm of VR makes these improbable feats possible.

5.7. The Future of Virtual Explorations

Despite the remarkable experiences offered by current VR technology, it is still in nascent stages in terms of potential. As we move forward, AI integration will enable more personalization and interactivity. Haptic technologies will allow us to touch and feel the virtual environments adding a tactile dimension. The distant vagueness of scents brought to life using olfactory technology can make these experiences even more realistic.

In conclusion, as VR technology evolves, the walls of reality will continue to blur. With VR in the realm of tourism, we're just beginning to scratch the surface of what is possible. The day isn't far when the physical presence at a location will be a choice, not a necessity, and exploring famous landmarks will just be a headset away.

Chapter 6. Into The Wild: Experiencing Exotic Destinations Virtually

The concept of virtual exploration has burgeoned into an innovative way of experiencing the world, offering an alternative to traditional travel. This chapter delves into the method of virtual tourism and encapsulates the ways in which you can traverse and explore the most exotic corners of the world without leaving your home.

6.1. Stepping Into The Virtual Environment

To start your virtual journey, a virtual reality headset is key. Oculus Rift, Samsung Gear VR, Google Cardboard, and PlayStation VR are among the frontrunners. Some require a smartphone to function, and others need to be connected to a gaming console or a computer. The growth in technology has also seen an improvement in VR resolution, providing a higher degree of immersion and a more visually exhilarating experience.

Once equipped with your VR gear, you can choose from the various VR platforms that facilitate virtual travel. Some popular options include Google Expeditions, YouVisit, and Explor VR.

6.2. Journey Through The Amazon Rainforest

Perhaps one of the most alluring virtual travel experiences is a journey through the rich biodiversity of the Amazon Rainforest. The VR tour mimics a genuine expedition, from the exhilaration of the river cruise to the fascination of observing its diverse flora and fauna.

With the interactive VR tour, you are not restrained by usual hiking trails. You'll puff your way virtually through dense foliage, gaze up at towering trees, and get nose-to-nose with an array of captivating animals - from sloths to vibrant parrots and fearsome jaguars. You'll experience the ecosystem transition from varied forest floors to a plethora of birds and tree-dwelling creatures inhabiting the canopy - a myriad of experiences previously unreachable on a traditional physical tour.

6.3. Sahara Desert: A Surreal Virtual Realm

Perhaps you are more drawn to the vast stretch of golden sands that is the Sahara Desert. With virtual travel, you can visit the world's largest hot desert and experience its attractions that would otherwise require days, if not weeks, to reach in person.

Explore the nomadic Bedouin lifestyle, relish virtual tagines prepared over a desert fire, and bed down for the night under a blanket of stars. Wander virtually through an oasis and learn about their lifeline in the desert. Virtual reality allows you to marvel at the Great Pyramids and decodable hieroglyphics without having to push through throngs of tourists - a feature especially valuable to those who face mobility barriers, financial constraints or other restrictions that would keep them from experiencing these wonders in person.

6.4. Virtual Escape to The Exotic Galapagos Islands

Approximately 1,000 km off the western coast of Ecuador, the volcanic Galapagos Islands captivate naturalists, geologists, and tourists worldwide. Virtual reality sweeps you up to this remote outpost - a hotspot of biodiversity including endemic species that exist nowhere else on Earth.

From the comfort of your home, bring to life the naturalist descriptions penned by Charles Darwin during his voyage on the HMS Beagle. Experience the interactions of fearless wildlife as you virtually snorkel with the marine creatures and stroll side-by-side with giant tortoises, sea lions, and penguins. Each island, each volcanic rock, each creature has a story to tell – all made possible through this innovation in virtual tourism.

6.5. The Ever-Enchanting Antarctican Landscape

Finally, brace yourself for a spine-tingling virtual encounter with Antarctica. Often seen as inaccessible due to its harsh climate and isolated location, Antarctica is now within reach through technology.

Conquer the sprawling ice sheets and iceberg-laden waters with virtual reality. Meet Emperor Penguins in colonies of thousands and watch seals lounging on ice floes. Listen to the silence, broken only by the occasional winds, penguin calls, and the creaking and groaning of ice. The glow of the midnight sun or the spectacular dance of the Aurora Australis can feel startlingly real with VR. The virtually recreated environment, curated based on real-life expeditions, offers an authentic polar experience that rivals those only described in expedition journals.

6.6. Conclusion

With virtual tourism, your quest for discovery is no longer bound by physical or financial constraints. The most exotic destinations, previously lying beyond the touch of everyday explorers, are now mere clicks away. Virtual reality has breathed a new life into travel and tourism, shaping the broad construct of future explorations. Dare to traipse into territory unknown to most, right from the threshold of your home.

Chapter 7. Behind The Scenes: Developing A VR Tour

The magic of VR tourism all begins from the perspiration and ambition of a dedicated team of experts, striving to transport you to world's afar from your living room.

7.1. The Beginning: Vision and Conception

Whether it's Venice, New Orleans, or the Northern Lights, the creation of a VR tour begins with a vision. Imagine a digital painter with a blank canvas, waiting to be filled with the intricate details of a city, natural landscape, or cultural event.

In this phase, team members brainstorm, sketch, and even take virtual or physical 'location scouting' trips to the chosen destination. From the broad cityscape down to the fluttering butterfly beside a historic monument, everything is considered, logged, and eventually translated into the virtual environment.

7.2. The Core Team: An Interdisciplinary Ensemble

To build such extensively detailed virtual experiences, a diverse team is assembled, including experts in 3D modeling, virtual reality programming, sound engineering, and even cultural advisors.

- The 3D modelers construct the digital landscapes, buildings, landmarks, and minor details within the VR tour.

- VR programmers develop the software that lets you navigate these terrains smoothly, ensuring a seamless and immersive experience.

- Sound engineers contribute to the ambiance, recreating the destination's auditory environment ranging from bustling city noises to soft nature sounds.

- Cultural advisors ensure the authenticity of the experience, contributing to the level of detail, accuracy, and respect towards the local culture.

7.3. The Gathering: Collation of Real-World Data

Creating an authentic VR tour involves extensive research and data collection. Coordination with tourism boards, historians, or local government is often necessary for access to maps, architectural sketches, and other resources. Drone footage and 3D scanning might be employed for detailed digital reproductions.

7.4. Modeling Reality: Creating the 3D Space

The creation of the 3D environment is where the collected data comes to life. The 3D modelers use the resource material to construct the landscape, including terrain, architecture, landmarks, objects, and people. This process is painstakingly detailed and lengthy, with a single building potentially taking up to several weeks to perfect.

7.5. The Nitty Gritty: Programming the VR Tour

The VR program is the backbone of the journey, guiding you through the 3D environment created. The programmers ensure you can move within this world smoothly, focusing on the development of intuitive controls and exploration mechanics.

7.6. Pumping Life: Dynamic and Interactive Elements

While the 3D space provides the foundation, the dynamic and interactive elements offer the fabric of life. Birds flying, water rippling, the hum of conversation from a café - details such as these provide depth and realism to the tour. The team also scripts interactions, allowing users to engage with their environment: open doors, pick up objects, or talk to locals.

7.7. Realistic Audio: Crafting the Sonic Environment

The sonic backdrop is an often overlooked but crucial part of the VR tour. The sound engineers aim to recreate the audio environment authentically, capturing and designing sounds ranging from the clamor of footsteps on cobblestones, local language chatter, or the echoing hush of a historic cathedral.

7.8. Testing and Refinement: Perfecting the Experience

Once the VR program is assembled, it undergoes rigorous testing. Tech experts, user experience designers, and even potential users are part of this process. Through this testing, issues related to motion sickness, navigation, interaction, and visual/audio realism are identified and rectified.

7.9. Final Thoughts

The creation of a VR tour isn't merely a technological enterprise. It's an interdisciplinary symphony, a collaboration of various people, and an effort towards recreating the human experience of a place in a digital environment. At its heart, VR tourism is about harnessing technology to build bridges between people and places, making the world a little smaller and more accessible. This is where the magic truly comes alive - turning pixels into experiences, and bits of data into memories.

Chapter 8. Couch Traveling: Benefits of Virtual Tourism

In an increasingly interconnected world, technology is persistently challenging perceptions and norms, creating opportunities to experience what was previously unimaginable. Nowhere is this more evident than in the realm of travel. Enter, Virtual Tourism. This burgeoning field leverages cutting-edge virtual reality (VR) to transport travel enthusiasts to far-flung corners of our planet from their own living rooms.

8.1. Understanding Virtual Tourism

Virtual Tourism, also referred to as couch traveling, stands at the intersection of technology and tourism—an innovative juncture where geographical boundaries cease to exist. Akin to teleportation in the realm of science fiction, it allows you to virtually 'visit' iconic world landmarks, hidden gems, or otherworldly landscapes with just the click of a button. The VR technology simulates your physical presence in these locations and enables you to interact and explore these places virtually. You can walk through the bustling streets of Tokyo, gaze in awe at the pyramids of Egypt, or wander in the wild expanses of African Savannah - a truly boundless experience.

8.2. The Technology Behind the Magic

The technology underpinning Virtual Tourism involves advanced VR systems comprising powerful software and hardware. The software creates immersive 360-degree video content, and the hardware—generally, a VR headset—generates a life-sized, 3D virtual environment without the boundaries typically seen on TV or computer screens. Advanced systems may include bodysuits or gloves with haptic feedback features, providing sensory input such as the feel of wind, water spray, or the sensation of touch, adding realism to the virtual journey.

8.3. Benefits of Virtual Tourism

In spite of seeming like a novelty, virtual tourism brings a slew of benefits to the table, transforming the way we approach travel and explore our world.

1. Accessibility: Physical constraints, health problems, or prohibitive costs can dissuade many from fulfilling their travel dreams. Couch traveling offers accessible means for anyone to explore global destinations, irrespective of their circumstances.

2. Education: From a virtual walk in the Amazon rainforest to a guided tour of the Louvre museum, VR experiences offer promising opportunities for immersive learning - a boon for students and curious minds alike.

3. Conservation: By offering virtual tours, we can relieve pressure on fragile ecosystems and historical sites facing risks from over-tourism, thus promoting responsible tourism.

4. Experimentation: Fear of the unknown can be a hindrance to travel. Virtual tourism allows people to 'try out' places, pushing their comfort zones, and inspiring them to plan real-world trips.

5. Time Saving: Bypass flight durations, layovers, or jet-lags; instantly satiate your travel cravings with couch travel.

8.4. A New Era of Sustainable Tourism

Virtual Tourism marks a shift in sustainable tourism practices. It presents an opportunity to democratize travel by making it more inclusive and accessible, without the negative impacts associated with mass tourism like environmental degradation, cultural erosion, strain on resources, and inflation.

8.5. Conclusion

As we sit poised on the brink of this exciting development, it's impossible not to be swept up in the potential it holds. Not only does it promise to broaden our horizons, deepen our empathy and understanding of diverse cultures, but it also puts us, as travelers, in a position of empowering sustainable travel practices. Virtual tourism represents a new chapter in the story of travel - one of inclusivity, accessibility, and sustainability, all while offering a tantalizing taste of the thrill and wonder that travel engenders.

In the context of recent global events, including the COVID-19 pandemic, understanding the role of Virtual Tourism has become particularly pertinent. As travel restrictions have constrained our movements, the ability to virtually explore the world offers a glimmer of light in a challenging time. By embracing technology's potential, we can continue to satisfy our wanderlust, while staying safe and responsible.

So, gear up, get your virtual reality headsets, and embark on an exhilarating journey to anywhere in the world you desire! As technology advances, there will only be more to see, do, and learn through this amazing avenue of virtual tourism. Shine a light on your travels ahead - all from the comfort of your couch!

Chapter 9. VR Technologies Transforming Tourism: Recent Innovations

Since the advent of virtual reality (VR) technology, there have been significant strides in various sectors, including tourism. It has emerged as a transformative tool that has redefined the very meaning of exploring the world. From giving users the ability to transport themselves to previously inaccessible locations to providing breathtaking panoramic views, VR offers the ultimate customizable travel experience.

9.1. Pioneering Virtual Reality Platforms in Tourism

Several VR platforms have been introduced in the tourism sector, each unique in its offerings, aimed to give users a reality-altering travel experience. Key players such as Google, Oculus, and Vive have contributed remarkable solutions through their VR platforms.

1. **Google Expeditions**: This app gives users a 360-degree view of hundreds of locations around the world, ranging from Great Barrier Reef to the Great Wall of China. A simple tap takes you to an immersive, lifelike simulation with interactive descriptions of historical and cultural elements of each destination.

2. **Oculus Go**: This completely wireless headset delivers a high-quality VR experience. Specifically curated experiences like 'Hulu VR' and 'National Geographic Explore VR' provide immersive mini-documentaries and scenic journeys across global destinations.

3. **HTC Vive**: Offering an immersive VR experience, the Vive comes

with a feature that lets users "walk around" in the VR world. It's particularly effective for exploring virtual replicas of tourist spots, creating a physically engaging and immersive experience.

9.2. Development of Virtual Tourism

As the VR technologies continue to expand and improve, so do the realm of virtual tourism experiences. We shall explore some of the recent innovations that are shaping the shift in how we travel virtually:

1. **Virtual Tours**: Many popular tourism locations, including world-famous museums like the Louvre and the British Museum, have initiated virtual tours of their establishments. Users can explore the location at their own pace, examining each exhibit to their heart's content without fighting tourist crowds.

2. **Virtual Reality Travel Agencies**: Companies like Ascape and YouVisit employ VR technology to allow potential tourists to sample locations before committing. This allows tourists to make informed decisions, improving their overall trip experience.

3. **Training and Education**: VR tourism isn't just for leisure. It's becoming a prevalent tool in education and training programs. Google Expedition, enhancing lessons with 360-degree VR experiences, takes students on field trips to virtually any location, providing a richer, more engaging learning experience.

4. **Marketing and Booking**: Businesses are using VR to promote destinations, providing potential customers a more interactive, immersive way to evaluate vacation spots. Examples include Marriott's Travel Brilliantly campaign and Kayak's VR Exploration Tool for booking.

9.3. Enhancing Accessibility through VR

VR technology has made the world more accessible, reducing barriers imposed by physical disability, age, and other constraints. Using VR, elderly people can virtually visit destinations they dreamed of, but their health constraints might not allow. Similarly, physically disabled people can experience the adventures from their homes that are challenging in the real world.

9.4. Conclusion: The Future of VR in Tourism

The marriage of VR and tourism isn't new, but recent advancements mark the beginning of a profound revolution in the way we experience travel. The future will see the evolution of VR-enriched travel, with more focused applications designed to hyper-personalize and enhance the traveler's experience.

However, even with its mounting success, the domain of VR is primarily a digital experience, lacking the tactile and sensory surprises that real-world travel delivers. As the technology continues to advance, we can expect to witness new developments that tackle this challenge and continue to blur the division between virtual and physical exploration.

This culminates our deep dive into how VR technology is transforming tourism and the recent innovations witnessed. The continuous development of VR points towards a future where anybody, anywhere can experience any corner of the globe, and that future is closer than we think.

Chapter 10. The Future Perspective: VR in Tourism Beyond 2022

In the world that is swiftly diving headlong into the digital wave, innovation never rests. As we look beyond 2022, it is clear that the potential and promise of Virtual Reality (VR) in the tourism sector is limitless. With continued technological advancement and ever-evolving consumer expectations, VR tourism is set to redefine our conception of travel, bringing new experiences and opportunities our way. This chapter seeks to unfold this future, delving into novel possibilities, the underlying challenges, and the next steps for the evolution of VR in tourism.

10.1. The Unfolding Possibilities

In the not-too-distant-future, virtual escapades will not merely be limited to sightseeing. With the integration of haptic feedback systems and advanced AI, travellers can look forward to immersive and interactive experiences.

Engaging AI-powered tour guides will be at your disposal, mimicking human-like interaction to guide you throughout your journey. Tour operators will pivot to including a variety of such immersive optional extras like guided digital tours, simulated local culinary tasting experiences, and interactive historical storytelling.

As software developers pair VR with haptic feedback, users will touch and physically interact with their surroundings. Imagine the sensation of treading on the gritty Moroccan sand dunes, feeling the spray of the Niagara Falls on your face, or the feeling of a snowflake melting in your hand in the Swiss Alps.

Moreover, multisensory VR experiences will let us cater to all senses. It is foreseeable that we will smell, taste, hear and feel the virtual world in addition to seeing it, making the tour surreal. This will elevate VR tourism to previously unreachable heights of authenticity and engagement.

10.2. Challenges Ahead

While the future of VR in tourism is teeming with promise, it is only fair to acknowledge the nuance of challenges it presents.

Foremost, addressing the 'Reality Paradox' - the wide gap between the experience in the actual versus virtual world - will be pivotal. Ensuring high-quality graphics, fluid motion, and sensory stimulation to emulate reality closely will be a marathon task.

Economically, the high cost of VR hardware may act as a barrier to widespread adoption of the technology. Furthermore, the continual need for software upgrades and equipment maintenance will incur constant expenses.

There could also be unintended social repercussions. As the allure of virtual worlds intensifies, the lines between reality and the virtual could blur, leading to increased screen-time and potential health-related repercussions.

10.3. Breaking New Ground: Collaborations and Partnerships

To overcome these hurdles, collaborations and partnerships will become even more crucial. Tech companies, gaming industries, tourism institutions, and regulatory bodies will need to work hand in hand to develop regulation, curb potential pitfalls, adapt according to user feedback, and work on making VR hardware more accessible.

Inter-industry collaborations could help in creating comprehensive solutions. For instance, partnership with medical and psychological experts can assist VR designers in creating safer and more health-conscious experiences. On a similar note, collaboration with educators can open doors to edutainment – a niche market for learning through travel experiences.

10.4. Preparing for the Revolution: Next Steps

While the revolution is inevitable, harnessing its potential requires preparation. Firstly, businesses must invest in training their employees about the new technology to integrate it smoothly into their landscape. Secondly, it is important to educate consumers about VR and its uses in tourism, encouraging its adoption.

On a larger scale, implementation of regulations and ethical guidelines will be necessary to ensure ethical use of VR and minimize potential negative impacts. Additionally, more funding should be funnelled into R&D for improving the technology and driving down costs.

10.5. Conclusion: Imagining a New Reality

As we stand on the precipice of a new travel era, the endless opportunities that VR provides are waiting to be exploited. It's high time to foster more innovation, collaboration, and preparedness to embrace this evolution. VR tourism is poised to make globe-trotters out of homebodies, and we look forward to this wonder-filled, fully immersive journey beyond 2022.

Chapter 11. Getting Started: Your Personal Guide to VR Tourism

Before we venture into the mesmerizing unknown of virtual reality tourism, it is imperative we familiarize ourselves with the fundamentals. This chapter serves as a thorough introduction to the virtual reality, the technology that makes it possible, and the endless new possibilities it offers in the realm of tourism.

11.1. VR Technology Explained

Virtual Reality (VR) is a computer-generated simulation of a three-dimensional environment that can be interacted with in a seemingly real or physical way. These interactions are typically conducted through specialized electronic equipment such as VR headsets, sensor-equipped gloves, or handheld controllers. The primary idea of VR is to create an immersive digital environment that you can experience just as you would the real world.

VR technology has evolved immensely over the last few decades, and today, you'll find two primary types of VR devices – standalone (like Oculus Quest) and tethered devices (like PlayStation VR). Standalone devices are self-contained units that don't require a PC or console to run, while tethered ones offer higher quality experiences, but need high-end PCs or consoles.

11.2. Setting Up Your VR Device

Buying and setting up a VR device doesn't have to be daunting. You can get up and running in just a few easy steps:

1. Purchase a VR headset that matches your requirements and budget. Consider factors such as resolution, field of view, refresh rate, and tethered or standalone.

2. Set it up according to the manufacturer's instructions. This typically involves connecting wires, placing sensors, and adjusting the fit for comfort.

3. Install any necessary software. This often means creating an account with the device's platform and downloading its app on your computer or phone.

4. Download VR experiences. Most VR devices come with a dedicated store filled with apps, games, and experiences for you to download.

5. Customize your settings. Test the device and adjust settings like brightness, sound, and movement controls to suit your preferences.

Remember, safety is paramount when using VR devices. Make sure your play area is clear, and take regular breaks to prevent fatigue or motion sickness.

11.3. VR Tourism: An Overview

While VR technology is prevalent in gaming, it is the potential it holds in transforming the tourism industry that is truly mind-boggling. VR tourism allows you to virtually explore a tourist attraction, city, or even an entire country without having to physically be there.

Imagine standing atop the Eiffel Tower, looking at Paris's sprawling cityscape, feeling the chill of the wind, hearing the city noises, all while you're actually in the confines of your house. Such is the power and promise of VR tourism.

Many famous museums, like the Louvre and the British Museum, national parks and World Heritage Sites have created virtual tours, enabling people from all over the world to explore and appreciate these sites without leaving their homes.

11.4. Choosing Your VR Travel Experiences

Just as you'd plan an actual itinerary, choose your virtual destinations based on your interests. Do you like hiking? Virtually scale Everest. Love wildlife? Explore the jungles of the Amazon. From exploring the sunken wrecks of the Titanic to observing the hustle-bustle of Tokyo, the possibilities are limitless.

Some virtual experiences are free to explore, while others come at a nominal cost. Remember, every experience may not be available on each VR platform, so it's essential to choose your VR equipment wisely.

11.5. Enhancing Your VR Travel Experience

A few tips to ensure you get the most out of your VR travels:

1. Engage fully: Treat your virtual tour as you would a real tour – soak in the sights, participate in guided tours, and ask questions if the platform allows.

2. Make it social: Invite friends and family to join you on your VR adventures. Many platforms allow for multi-user experiences, making it possible to travel with loved ones in the virtual space.

3. Experience the culture: Attend virtual concerts, try virtual cooking lessons, or participate in traditional ceremonies - engage as much as you can with local culture.

In conclusion, your journey into VR tourism is just beginning, and with this guide, you're equipped with a powerful new tool that lets you experience the wonders of the planet, no matter where you are. Happy virtual traveling!